Drinking Water

by Helen Frost

Consulting Editor: Gail Saunders-Smith, Ph.D.

Consultant: Linda Hathaway
Health Educator
McMillen Center for Health Education

Pebble Books

an imprint of Capstone Press
Mankato, Minnesota

Pebble Books are published by Capstone Press
151 Good Counsel Drive, P.O. Box 669, Mankato, Minnesota 56002
http://www.capstone-press.com

1 2 3 4 5 6 05 04 03 02 01 00

Library of Congress Cataloging-in-Publication Data
Frost, Helen, 1949–
    Drinking water/by Helen Frost.
    p. cm.—(Food guide pyramid)
    Includes bibliographical references and index.
    Summary: Text and photographs show what water does in the body and why it
is essential to our health.
    ISBN 0-7368-0534-6
    1. Water—Physiological effect—Juvenile literature. {1. Water.} I. Title. II. Series.
QP535.H1 F76   2000
612′.01522—dc21   99-05692

Note to Parents and Teachers

The Food Guide Pyramid series supports national science standards related to physical health and nutrition. This book describes and illustrates the importance of drinking water. The photographs support early readers in understanding the text. The repetition of words and phrases helps early readers learn new words. This book also introduces early readers to subject-specific vocabulary words, which are defined in the Words to Know section. Early readers may need assistance to read some words and to use the Table of Contents, Words to Know, Read More, Internet Sites, and Index/Word List sections of the book.

Table of Contents

4

You need to drink
water to stay healthy.

Water keeps your body working well.

Water helps
you digest food.

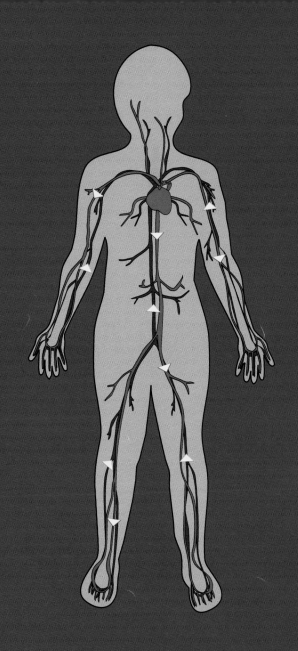

10

Water helps move nutrients through your body.

More than half of your body weight is water. Drinking enough water keeps you healthy.

14

You need to drink more water when you are active.

You need to drink more water when you are hot.

The water you drink
keeps you cool.

You should drink at least eight glasses of water every day.

Words to Know

digest—to break down food for use in your body; your body digests food to gain energy.

energy—the strength to be active without becoming tired

food—items people eat to stay alive and grow; most food has water in it.

healthy—fit and well; drinking at least eight 8-ounce (170-gram) glasses of water every day keeps you healthy.

nutrients—something that people, plants, and animals need to stay healthy; water helps move nutrients through your body.

Read More

Frost, Helen. *We Need Water.* Water. Mankato, Minn.: Pebble Books, 2000.

Hooper, Meredith, and Chris Coady. *The Drop in My Drink: The Story of Water on Our Planet.* New York: Viking, 1998.

Kalbacken, Joan. *The Food Pyramid.* A True Book. New York: Children's Press, 1998.

Rockwell, Lizzy. *Good Enough to Eat.* A Kid's Guide to Food and Nutrition. New York: HarperCollins, 1999.

Internet Sites

Drinking Water: Kids' Stuff
http://www.epa.gov/OGWDW/kids

Drink Up! Why Water Is the Way to Go
http://www.kidshealth.org/kid/food/water.html

Water Myths and Realities
http://www.awwa.org/watermyt.htm

Index/Word List

Word Count: 79
Early-Intervention Level: 9

Editorial Credits
Mari C. Schuh, editor; Heather Kindseth, cover designer; Sara A. Sinnard, illustrator; Kia Bielke, illustrator; Kimberly Danger, photo researcher

Photo Credits
David F. Clobes, cover
Index Stock Imagery, 12
International Stock/Laurie Bayer, 8
Jim Cummins/FPG International LLC, 16
Kim Stanton, 18
Leslie O'Shaughnessy, 1
Matt Swinden, 20
Photo Agora/Larry Javorsky, 4
Richard B. Levine, 14
Uniphoto/Lee Klopfer, 6